MICROCOSM

Microcosm is Portland's autistic-owned and most diversified publishing house and distributor with a focus on the colorful, authentic, and empowering. Our books and zines have put your power in your hands since 1996, equipping readers to make positive changes in their lives and in the world around them. Microcosm emphasizes skill-building, showing hidden histories, and fostering creativity through challenging conventional publishing wisdom with books and bookettes about DIY skills, food, bicycling, gender, self-care, and social justice.

INTRODUCTION
WHAT IS CONSENT AND WHY DO WE NEED TO DISCUSS IT?

onsent is *the informed, voluntary permission given or agreement reached for an activity/exchange between two or more sentient beings.* When it comes to the expression and negotiation of our boundaries, we generally do so through how we communicate consent. If someone asks you "Hey, can I borrow this book?" they are recognizing that the book is something you own (property boundary!), and asking if they can use yonur book and return it (consent for exchange!)

So you might ask, if everyone and their labradoodle is talking about consent these days, why is this zine different and special?

You ask great questions, thank you for that.

I've been teaching consent workshops for years now, far longer than consent has been a cultural buzzword. Consent and boundaries issues are an almost universal concern for the individuals I've worked with in therapy and I've heard the same thing from my colleagues. Because consent is something that we suck at, culturally. So I was always trying to find ways to re-center it. This meant paying attention to all the different topics that I write about in this zine—many of which aren't being discussed in other spaces. Because I've found that *all* of these topics are important to creating lasting cultural change.

So that means we gotta talk about the history of consent and respecting personhood (like, starting back thousands of years ago... because context is important and I know you're a big nerd like I am). Then we are going to demystify all the words and acronyms around consent (because what the fuck is a RACK, anyway?), and because it's is really fucking important...we are going to go into the legal issues that we bump into around consent.

But, wait! That's not all! There is not a free set of Ginzu knives included (Microcosm did not consent to the shipping costs involved), but I am going to talk about rape culture and #metoo. Because that's the reality of what we are up against and why this cultural shift feels like trying to change deck chairs on the Titanic.

And since it's a hard-core battle with few useful tools, I'm including some fucking useful tools. I have a lot of sample guidelines for creating consent based interpersonal interactions and group norms... which is a fancy way of saying setting good boundaries around consent whether with one person or many. And since boundaries are the everyday expression of consent (which you know if you read my boundaries book), there are some exercises relating specifically to how we manage and express those aforementioned boundaries.

Yeah, that's a lot. And it's not light-hearted insta-inspo mantra messages about consent that feel good but don't get the work done. We're all here to actually change shit. So take care of yourself. Difficult work is called difficult for a damn reason. World-changing is exhausting, but necessary. I'm glad you're in it with me.

THE HISTORY OF CONSENT
From Biblical to Modern Times

Here in the early 21st century, we understand consent stemming from the assumption that all of us (at least in theory) have bodily autonomy. Meaning that we have ownership of our own bodies and get to make decisions about them. And that seems like one of those self-evident truths, but many times and places throughout human history (especially European history, which tends to be our cultural paradigm set-point), that was NOT a given.

In ancient (human) history, only people with power and wealth were considered to have autonomy (sound familiar?). The expectation was that those people would act in the best interests of all the poor people under their rule (sooooo familiar!). We saw this time and again in the texts of Plato, Hippocrates, and the like in ancient European history.

By contrast, some other ancient texts, like those from Buddhist, Jaina, and Hindu history, called out the powerful to attend to the inherent ethical responsibility we have to respect one another (early Twitter drags?). But these religious schools of thought did not have much impact on our modern, industrial society (yep, definitely early Twitter drags).

The first cultural shift in European thought started with early Christianity. Augustine's criticism of unjust political authority in the 4th century was a huge change in thinking about the issue. He wasn't setting out to produce political commentary, but to hold humanity to a higher authority, but in doing so questioned the all-powerful nature of a political regime to make decisions for its people, by challenging power structures by examining the work they are doing . One could make an effective argument that Augustine started the movement toward autonomy and consent when he said *"Remove justice and what are kingdoms but gangs of criminals on a large scale? What are criminal gangs but petty kingdoms?"* The idea that power structures should serve a greater good, rather than of their own accord and to their sole benefit was seriously, incredibly radical shit at the time. It meant that all of society should consent to, and benefit from, the decisions that leaders in power were making.

And then Immanual Kant came along in the 18th century, and shifted philosophical thought even further by arguing a moral philosophy of individual personhood. Meaning, we exist in and of ourselves with motivations that are unique to us that should not be forced upon us by external forces.

These two ideas, that those in power should serve everyone and everyone has an autonomous existence, that should seem completely "well, duh" to anyone with a brain are actually pretty new. Thanks to Kant and Augustine, we added "people get to be who they are" and "systems designed to support people should have everyone's interests, not their own and aren't allowed to do fucked up shit just because they can" to the social conscious.

Don't get me wrong, humans still sucked at actually obtaining consent from people...but at least the idea that we SHOULD was starting to sink in.

Consent in the Modern Era

The concept of affirmative consent is often attributed to the authors of a policy put in place at Antioch College in 1991. It was a response to two occurrences of rape on the campus that year and a need for a more inclusive sexual misconduct policy. The policy spelled out that during sexual activity, everyone involved must give verbal consent to each sexual activity that was was being considered. Oral sex wasn't consent for anal sex, and sex on Tuesday was not consent for sex on Friday. It was met with great derision from the media...including an SNL skit that made fun of it (still findable on YouTube if you aren't old enough to remember it).

But actually, the idea of affirmative consent predates Antioch College by a few years...and it comes from the kink community.

As HIV gained more awareness, BDSM communities started writing rules on *asking permission.* In 1981 the first formal bylaws regarding affirmative consent were written by members of a New York leather collective known as the Gay Male S/M Collective (GMSMC). They coined the term "safe, sane, and consensual," a concept that is still used within the kink community (for other consent related terms that have been embraced by kink communities, check out the appendix). Their work has been continued through the National Coalition on Sexual Freedom's Consent Counts Program. The Consent Counts Program currently defines consent as:

For our purposes, consent is the explicit indication, by written or oral statement, by one person that they are willing to have something done to them by one or more other persons, or to perform some sort of act at the request or order of one or more other persons. In terms of sexual consent, consent may be withdrawn at any point, regardless of what has been previously negotiated orally or in writing.

The work of the kink community and Antioch college are the underpinnings of the letter the Obama administration sent out to 7000 college campuses in 2011, challenging how sexual assault assaults were investigated by universities under Title IX. This letter, coupled with the Clery Act, a consumer protection act regarding campus safety and crime policies, started a shift in how we started to view consent and respond to violations of consent. In 2017, the state of California implemented a law requiring students in all grades to receive information on consent.

There has also been a radical shift in how we view consent in the medical community in recent years. As a mental health practitioner, I include a dialogue about informed consent as an essential part of the intake process. The US government's FDA.gov's clearinghouse notes that informed consent is more than just a signature on a form, it is a process of information exchange." This is a vital framework for everything else we are discussing.

The Australian medical establishment started making huge changes in the aughts related to how informed consent was framed, changes that could make a huge, positive impact on society if we challenge ourselves to use them. In the past, informed consent for treatment in England and Australia was based on something termed the Bolam test. The Bolam test (the term refers to a court case from 1957) meant that practitioners are not negligent in their informed consent practices as long as they are acting within the current practice of medical opinion. Essentially, if the medical establishment maintains that how you are obtaining consent for treatment is good enough, then the court system agreed that it is, in fact, good enough.

The legal community in both countries started to challenge that, saying it's not so much what doctors as a whole think is reasonable that matters, it's what patients as a whole think is reasonable. They are the people from which we are securing consent...and the opinion of the giver means more than the opinion of the taker. And there are certain factors that need to be taken into consideration that include:

1) The nature of the matter at hand. The more serious the possible consequences, the more discussion needs to happen.

2) The complexity of the proposed interaction. The more complex the procedure, the more information needs to be given. And for things that don't need to happen (in this case, elective procedures), the more information needs to be given.

3) The giver's desire for information. If people have questions about what is being proposed, those questions need to be answered fully and not dismissed as unnecessary.

4) The giver's temperament and health. Relevant circumstances need to be addressed. If someone is anxious, they likely need more information. If their situation is complicated and other factors may present a risk they need information about that.

Doctors are now being held as *negligent* when their consent procedures do not match what a reasonable patient would expect. The court system is less and less concerned about what reasonable doctors, their peers, would expect. Some of the findings of neglect include a doctor not disclosing the possibility of getting an inflammatory disease from the insertion of an IUD or of suffering nerve damage due to the removal of a lymph node. And I think we can all agree that that is important information that patients should have.

But shouldn't the same standard apply to all of our consent-requesting conversations? You'll notice that I described these four factors in a general way, outside of just medical treatment consent. And that's because they are super relevant to all forms of consent, not just medical treatment. For example, with number 4? In a medical consent situation it may be letting someone know that a surgery they are considering may have outcomes that are affected because the patient is also diabetic. In a regular life situation, it may be letting someone know that you want to borrow their car but may not get it back in time for them to use it to get to work.

TYPES OF CONSENT

We've started having more conversations around sexual consent in recent years (yaaay!) but they have been pretty stuck in a thematic loop of "active continuous consent or nothing!!!" when in reality it's far more complicated than that. Having real discussions around consent means understanding our cultural norms (and dismantling the fuck out of them as needed).

Originating Consent is a philosophy term that refers to our cultural standards of acceptable behaviors. It's the societal understanding of what is a legitimate and appropriate practice and what is not. Originating consent is fluid, as cultural context is ever-changing. What that means is that our laws come into effect based on our cultural standards of being good humans to each other.

Shifts are made when people start saying "What the fuck is up with this?" and laws are put into place to back that up. Laws, ethical standards, and the like are almost always *historical*. Meaning, we create them when we realize there is a problem that needs to be addressed. In England, it became against the law in 1275 to "ravish" a maiden (with or without her consent) if she was not of marriageable age (which was 12). That's when social norms of originating consent were formalized into laws. The law about raping children was formalized once people realized that raping children was a problem that couldn't be ignored.

Far more recent example: the term *upskirting* refers to the practice of taking photos or videos of someone literally up their skirt without their consent. In 2016, a grocery store clerk named Brandon Lee Gary went to trial for doing exactly this to a woman who was shopping at the store he worked at. His conviction was overturned in appeals because the law didn't reflect the illegality of this boundary violation (technology allows for creativity in shitty behavior). Courts don't make the laws, they only interpret and uphold them...so the Georgia legislature passed a bill into law the next year making upskirting illegal.

Originating consent is an important part of any boundary conversation because that's where cultural shifts are recognized and formalized into law as need be. You've heard the term *consent culture*, right? Consent culture is the normalization of asking for consent for interaction with others. For being disappointed but not butthurt when someone says no. Consent culture at its highest level-up is when we don't feel weird or embarrassed for establishing and respecting boundaries. Our shift to consent culture means we are shifting our understanding of originating consent. And as our thinking shifts, our laws are starting to reflect these ideals.

About motherfucking time.

Ok, so now that we've all earned an advanced degree in philosophy, let's talk about what originating consent looks like in practice.

Permissive consent is another term from those wild kids in the philosophy department. Permissive consent is what allows us to engage in specific actions in relation to those cultural standards of practice and social norms. For example, originating consent holds that it is not acceptable behavior to stab needles into another human being on the regular, right? But if you go see a tattoo artist, sign their waiver, and pay them for their work, you are engaging in *permissive consent*.

Permissive consent is our expression of boundaries in context. And despite all our conversations about active, continuous consent the reality is that most consent is *not* verbal. This isn't good or bad, it's just something to be aware of.

Permissive consent is established in one of three ways:

- **Explicit Consent:** Explicit consent requires the "yes" to be spoken. It is directly expressed consent. A contract that is reviewed, understood, and signed before any exchange is explicit consent. Asking another person "may I -------- your --------" is explicit consent. When we talk about active, continuous consent (meaning active agreement to activity with continued check-ins that the activity is still a go) we are talking about explicit consent.

- **Implicit Consent:** Implicit consent operates on presumptions of nos and yeses. It is the inference of consent based on our actions and circumstances. This isn't a fundamentally terrible thing. We do it all the time. If I purchase a bag of pistachios and leave it on my husband's desk, the implication is that they are there for him to eat. If you apply for a job and your resume includes the names and contact information for references, the implication is that the potential employer will call them to verify your employment eligibility. This is also the area that gets people in the most trouble, such as when someone presumes that engaging in one sexual activity implies consent for another activity that wasn't discussed.

- **Blanket/Opt-Out/Meta-Consent:** These types of consent require a "no" to be spoken. They give the opportunity for the no and if the no is not forthcoming, the "yes" is presumed. This is another common way of operating within close relationships. For example, someone you know well may hug you when they see you and the presumption would be that that is a norm in your relationship. If you weren't down for a hug, you would say "I'm super touched out today, I need a mulligan on the hug" to let them know there was a change in your normal interactions. An example within the BDSM community would be in edge play, where the dom is setting the scene but the sub has a safeword that they can invoke.

Questions for Reflection

- Where are some areas where we have failed as a culture in providing healthy originating consent?

- What are some avenues to start creating a cultural shift in that regard (activism alert!!!!)?

- Which types of permissive consent do you prefer?

- How do you typically communicate explicit consent verbally? Nonverbally?

- Which people do you feel comfortable operating with implicit and/or blanket consent?

- How do you communicate when there was an error in someone's presumption of implicit consent?

- How do you communicate your opt-out in blanket consent?

- Which people in your life (past and present) are good at respecting your boundaries and gaining consent?

- Which people in your life (past and present) struggle to respect your boundaries and consent?

- How do you recognize hesitation in someone else's language or body?

- Which people who are currently present in your life that you need to work with reestablishing better expressions of consent?

Some Consent Terminology

Just like consent in general, these terms were born within kink communities but are hugely beneficial in all kinds of situations and interactions.

- **Age of Consent:** Age of consent is a legal term that varies in different countries and in different states or regions of different countries. It refers to the legal age an individual must be before they can legally engage in and consent to sexual activity. In some countries (like Bolivia), the age of consent corresponds with puberty. In others the law requires older adolescence, such as in the United States where it lies between ages 16 and 18, depending on the state. There are sometimes exceptions to age of consent laws, such as for marriage.

- **Capacity to Consent:** Capacity to consent refers to an individual's ability to understand and make and communicate decisions regarding activities they wish to engage in. Someone may say "yes" to an activity but may not have the capacity to take responsibility for that "yes" if they are under the influence, or have certain developmental limitations or mental health issues.

- **Informed Consent:** Informed consent refers to the consent that is given freely and willingly by another party once they have been given all pertinent information about what they are agreeing to, before the action takes place, without any pressure, coercion, or misrepresentation of the situation.

You must also be of age of consent and with the capacity to consent in order to give informed consent.

...and some BDSM specific consent terms....

- **Good, Giving, and Game (GGG) -** Good, giving, and game (GGG) is a term that was coined by Dan Savage, a US writer with an internationally syndicated sex column. This term describes individuals who have no problem expressing their sexuality and are willing to try new things, within reason and with the expectation that boundaries are respected. GGG folks have worked through previous negative messages about sex and embrace sexual pleasure as a rightful part of their lives. Outside of sexual interactions, being a GGG person means embracing all the unique qualities that make you who you are, not being ashamed of your quirks, not being interested in towing the party line, and finding the people with whom you can connect authentically. GGG people are not ashamed of geeking out over the current season of Dr. Who or a new recording of Wagner's Der Ring des Nibelungen. You do you.

- **Safe, Sane, Consensual (SSC) -** Another alternative sexuality community term referring to the components required for consent. SSC was adopted by the BDSM community to differentiate between BDSM and abuse. Safe means that all risks involved in the interaction are understood by all parties and everything possible is done to reduce or eliminate those risks. Sane means that everything engaged in is done so in a realistic way, and everyone can effectively differentiate between fantasy and reality. And consensual remains the basis of all interaction—that all participants were in an appropriate frame of mine to explicitly consent to the activities being engaged in. SSC easily applies to all relationships, not just sexual ones, because the fundamental message is to be mindful and thoughtful in our interactions with people.

- **Risk Aware Consensual Kink (RACK) -** The term RACK evolved as a response to the term SSC in order to include the recognition that some BDSM activities are not always risk-free. RACK encourages personal accountability for the risks inherent in some BDSM activities. While I would make the argument that just living life is risky and we should all be risk-mindful, RACK is generally used in regards to edgeplay and other BDSM activities with a higher likelihood of risk. For this reason the National Coalition on Sexual Freedom (NCSF) warns that there are potential legal problems with the use of the term. If a scene architect uses the term RACK in pre-scene planning, the concern is that they are acknowledging risk of harm in a way that creates legal liability for them if something does go wrong.

- **Personal Responsibility, Informed, Consensual Kink (PRICK) -** PRICK became a more common term around 2009, according to the website Kinkly, as part of a response to concerns around the acronym RACK. While similar, PRICK centers the responsibility and consequences upon risky behavior upon the person taking the risk in consensual exchanges. Pushback regarding this term included the argument that if you are new to a certain activity, you can't be completely informed, especially regarding your emotional response to activities in which you chose to engage.

SEXUAL VIOLENCE, GENDER, & #METOO

I f we are going to talk about consent, we have to talk about rape culture. I'd rather talk about anything other than rape culture, and I imagine you would, too. But neither of us are going to shy away from the tough conversations we need to have in order to change the world and heal our own lives. Talking about the shit we don't want to talk about takes it out of the shadows so we can really face it and transform it. So let's wear our grown-up pants and call it what it is.

We live in a rape culture, not a consent culture. Rape culture is a term that refers to a norm regarding sexual violence. Meaning the general social attitudes and practices tolerate, excuse, condone, and even glamorize sexual violence. We have seen case after case of young men being given light sentences for sexual assault because they had "bright futures" that the judge didn't want to "ruin" (People Vs. Turner is the biggest recent example). Tolerating, excusing and condoning right there.

Yeah, Faith. But *glamorizing*? We aren't that fucked up, are we? If you haven't seen the 1984 movie *Revenge of the Nerds* go check out the moon bounce scene. I'm sure it's on YouTube. One character pretends to be the boyfriend of the other and has sex with her. When he is later unmasked, he *gets the girl* because the sex was so good. That was over thirty years ago, though right?

But a similar storyline played out in Season 3 of the TV show *Younger* in 2016 where Hillary Duff's character finds out that her late fiancee's twin brother had pretended to be her fiance in order to have sex with her. He didn't keep the girl, but the storyline was granted no more than an "ew" by the characters. (And mad props to Mr. Dr. Faith, who is Woke Bae (™), because he was screaming at the television "CALL IT RAPE FOR FUCK'S SAKE WHY IS HE NOT GOING TO JAIL?" Rape as an amusing plot point: that's the glamorization of rape culture in a nutshell.

The original #MeToo movement was founded by Tarana Burke in 2006, and was designed to provide affirming space for people to talk about the sexual abuse and harrassment that they have experienced. It came into the national consciousness in 2017 with the viral hashtag #metoo, following a flood of allegations of sexual abuse against film producer Harvey Weinstein.

The hashtag says it all doesn't it? It illuminates how universal sexual violence is in our society and gives voice to that experience. There is a saying in 12 step recovery: *You are only as sick as your secrets.* When we stop being ashamed of being victims, we can heal, as people and as a society. Healing doesn't erase our trauma, but it transforms victimhood into survivorship. And without this transformation, it's pretty impossible to move forward, living in relationships where healthy boundaries provide our blueprint for connection.

Violence, overall, is gendered. The best way to predict if someone is likely to be violent is not if they are a person of color, or poor, but simply if they are male or not. The best-studied form of gendered violence is sexual assault, and even so, these are horrifically underreported. And yes, men are absolutely victims of sexual violence as well, almost always victimized by other men. When we look at the statistic compiled by the National Sexual Violence Resource Center, the first one that jumps out is this: *1 in 5 women and 1 in 71 men will be raped at some point in their lives.*

And we say, yeah, that's pretty fucked up. But men aren't victimized by other men at nearly the same rate. I mean, there's a big difference between 20% of women and 1% of men. Until you realize that rape is only one form of sexual violence. Let's look at some other statistics.

46.4% lesbians, 74.9% bisexual women and 43.3% heterosexual women reported sexual violence other than rape during their lifetimes, while 40.2% gay men, 47.4% bisexual men and 20.8% heterosexual men reported sexual violence other than rape during their lifetimes. Gay and plurisexual individuals are at high risk for sexual violence, regardless of their gender. And when it comes to sexua violence in general, straight dudes also hit that 20% statistic once we look at sexual violence in general, not just rape.

The rate of sexual violence against non-cis people is even more horrific. According to the 2015 U.S. Transgender Survey Report, 47% of the respondents were sexually assaulted at some point in their lifetime, 10% had been sexually assaulted in the past year and the numbers were even higher among trans folks of color. When those numbers are broken down, transgender men and nonbinary individuals who have vaginas were more likely to be sexually assaulted than transgender women and nonbinary individuals who have penii, reinforcing the notion that the individuals with a vagina are still at the highest level of risk.

Childhood sexual abuse numbers are even more devastating. One in four girls and one in six boys will be sexually abused before they turn 18. The average age of victimization is lower for boys instead of girls. Boys are more likely to be victimized before they are even ten years old.

And no matter the victim's gender, the perpetrator is nearly always a man. The Department of Justice notes that 99% of individuals arrested for rape are men. 96% of individuals guilty of childhood sexual abuse are male, and about 75% of them are adult men.

This begs the question: Why is violence, especially sexual violence, gendered? Are men just naturally more aggressive and violent than women? Of course not. It means that our social norms operate as incubators for men's violent behaviors and men, women, boys, girls, and nonbinary individuals are all at risk.

A study conducted by researchers at the University Of North Dakota found that 1 out of 3 college men stated that they would rape a woman if they knew they could get away with it, so long as you took the ugly word "rape" out of the question. When the term was "intentions to rape a woman," 13.6% agreed that they would do so (still scary). But when the term was "intentions to force a woman to sexual intercourse," the number jumped to 31.7%. ***One in three.***

And yes, totally, this was one small study of 73 people which isn't indicative of how all men think. But even as a small snapshot of one particular group of men in one particular location, it's scary as fuck.

Culturally, we don't like the word rape. But we continue to perpetuate a social system in which non-consensual sexual acts are excused, dismissed, justified, minimized, and even glorified.

Social Norms that Perpetuate Rape
- Misogynistic language
- Fetishizing language
- The objectification of people's bodies

- Sexually explicit jokes that are dismissed as "locker room talk" and the like
- Tolerance of sexual harassment
- Victim blaming
- Victim dismissal
- Not taking rape accusations seriously
- Focusing prevention tactics around teaching potential victims on how to not be raped, rather than on preventing perpetration of rape.
- Scrutiny of a victim's behavior during the assault or past behavior (how they dressed, mental state, intoxicant usage, motives, and history (especially their sexual history)
- Inflating false rape report statistics
- Media centering of false rape report stories
- Trivializing sexual assault ("boys will be boys")
- Trivializing sexual harassment ("he was just giving you a compliment")
- Gratuitious sexual violence in movies, TV, and other media
- Defining "manhood" as dominant and sexually aggressive
- Pressuring men to "score"
- Defining "womanhood" as submissive and sexually passive
- Pressuring women to play "hard to get" and "need convincing"
- Assuming people only get raped if they put themselves in dangerous situations or engage in promiscuous behavior
- Assuming then men don't get raped, or only weak men get raped.

- Assuming that trans and nonbinary individuals don't get raped.

- Assuming that sex workers can't be raped

- Assuming that someone who is married or in a romantic relationship cannot be raped by another person in that relationship.

Rape culture is the literal opposite of consent culture. If consent is how we convey boundaries then it's no wonder that rape culture has kneecapped any dialogue or standards of personal boundaries.

In consent culture, only yes means yes. Accepting this means that many people have to revisit past behaviors, to consider that maybe some past actions were actually violations, not "grey areas." Rape culture is essentially a *justification culture,* whereas consent culture means we, all of us, are entirely responsible for our behavior at all times. No excuses. As Cristien Storm affirms on the very first page in her wonderful book *Empowered Boundaries, "the very act of boundary setting is political whether we like it or not."*

Politics is overwhelming. It's fucking awful and confusing and unending. I understand the desire to disconnect from the political nature of society, and you might be wondering why I am dragging politics into a mental health topic.

Respecting boundaries means respecting personhood. But the minute we start saying **"I, too, have a personhood to be respected"** through the act of establishing and communicating boundaries, we are changing our relationships and our expectations of interactions within our surrounding community. We are evolving our concept of originating consent for the betterment of all humans. All equal rights movements started with the statement of a boundary. Abolition, voting rights, desegregation, freedom to marry who you love.

No matter how apolitical you may be in other domains, the minute you start fighting for the establishment and recognition of your boundaries and the boundaries of others you have become political revolutionary. Welcome to the team.

Questions for Consideration

1) What community/social structures do you operate within that have impacted your ability to articulate your individual boundaries with the expectation of having them respected?

2) Has that changed any as you have gotten older? How so?

3) What kind of response do you anticipate when you chall

THE CONSENT COMMANDMENTS

onsent is an active process of communication. It's not just the *"can I [blank] this part of your body with [blank] part of my body"* that we see repeated ad nauseum in mainstream media. It's just as much my cat flattening her ears when she doesn't want pickie-uppies. Or my husband scrunching his face when I even *think* about putting onions in whatever I'm cooking.

At its core, consent is simply *permission for something to happen*. Consent defines our rules of engagement, the ones we express through boundaries.

We have all had experiences where our boundaries were violated and others did not request permission to interact with us, especially in regard to sex and intimacy. I am continuously surprised/not surprised by how often my fellow clinicians in the field, even, misunderstand the need for active consent in relationships. We presume that permission for one activity implies permission for others.

Consent provides a safe framework for interactions. For those of us with trauma histories, a safe framework can be a very healing experience. And, equally important, it allows us to experience own our desires in a sex-positive way. In an ideal situation, you aren't having to be convinced, you're saying *yes!*

These ten commandments came from a class I was teaching a few years ago for clinicians working with teens. We walked through group activities they could use to teach consent and boundaries *and* work with issues related to boundary violations. When it comes down to the basics, however, there are some fundamentals that apply universally. And as a good preacher's kid, I dug the idea of some basic commandments. Just like the OG commandments that Moses lugged down on stone tablets, they operate as a guide for our relational interactions, without weighing near as much, thankfully.

1. Consent for sex (and any other behaviors you are asking someone to engage in) cannot be given by people who are drunk. Or under the influence of drugs. Or hardcore medications. People under the influence are already doing seriously dumb stuff, like craving those two for a dollar tacos from Jack in the Box. So don't add something to their regret list that has large, long-term consequences.

2. Going through a lot of emotional stuff can be just as bad for your decision-making process as being drunk. If someone is stressed out or dealing with a lot, they may be seeking comfort and connection, and we often equate that with sex. If you think someone isn't making a good decision, put sex on hold and be there for them in other ways—like ones that won't embarrass them a week from now.

3. Consent isn't static. Agreeing to something on one occasion does not mean agreeing to it forever. So I let you borrow my car last week. Maybe you brought it back with the gas tank empty and full of used Starbucks cups and candy wrappers and I don't want you using it again. Maybe you took fantastic care of it, but I still don't want you using it again. Either way, it's still my car, not yours. You don't just march in my house, grab the keys off the counter, and take off in my car because I let you do it last week. No consent equals Grand Theft Auto, right?

4. Consent for one thing isn't consent for another. Someone gets naked in front of you? This is an excellent sign, yes. Is it consent for any specific sexual activity? No. Agreeing to one kind of activity isn't agreeing to all of them. Making out doesn't mean oral sex is cool. And yes to oral sex doesn't mean yes to penetrative sex. Our interactions are a salad bar, not a casserole. Wanting croutons doesn't mean you also have to have bell peppers, yanno?

5. Silence isn't consent. Someone may not actively say "no," but being passive isn't a "yes." Many times individuals don't speak up because they are freaked out or don't know how to. They could be quietly unhappy or quietly enjoying themselves. You don't know if you don't ask.

6. Consent needs to be informed. Are you sleeping with other people? That's ok, it's called dating not getting married for a reason. Have a sexually transmitted infection? That happens, too. Moving out of state in a week? That can impact future plans a bit. Potential partners need to know all of the above and any other information that may inform their decision about sexual activity. Be grown-up enough to have the awkward conversations.

7. Consent is a community obligation, not just a personal one. We need to help support each other with gray areas of consent. Speak up if you see someone in an uncomfortable situation and back up their right to say no. Friends don't let friends listen to Nickelback, and they don't let them get into situations where they are not really giving consent or not really getting consent. If you see someone at a party getting into a danger zone, then be the protective wingperson. And if the DJ plays Nickelback, it's time to leave altogether.

8. Having to convince someone is not consent. You aren't trying to win a court case by wooing a jury member. You're awesome, right? If they aren't into you enough to realize that and you have to convince them, then they don't deserve your awesomeness. If you get a "Wellllllllll, I don't knowwwwww," respond with, "That's cool, let me know if you change your mind" and then step away from the sex.

9. Consent doesn't just mean the right to say no, it also means the right to say *yes*. Shaming people because they choose to engage in sexual activity makes active, enthusiastic consent way more complicated. Affirmative consent is difficult for many people (usually women) because they think that an enthusiastic yes means they are slutty, and that they

are supposed to pretend they *don't* want sex and must be "convinced." This sends mixed messages to their partners. When are we supposed to "convince" and when are we supposed to just stop? If everyone is sexually empowered, no one ever has to be "convinced."

10. Consent is more than just sex, it's about boundaries in general. You should get people's permission to touch them for any reason (e.g., "You look like you could use a hug right now, would you like one?"). Consent extends past physical boundaries, as well. You should never force your will on others. Don't share others' information, experiences, images, or things without their permission. Don't make plans on their behalf without their permission. Don't force them to share information with you or anyone else if they are uncomfortable doing so. No matter what you think is in their best interest, unless you are their legal guardian, let them make their own decisions. You do you and let them be them.

THE WHEEL OF CONSENT

The concept of the Wheel of Consent is the brainchild of Betty Martin. She uses it to help individuals frame their experience of touch, and it's an amazing exercise in that regard. For the purposes of this book, I've expanded her wheel out to encompass all aspects of consent, not just consent for touch.

You can use the wheel to reflect on and unpack your past experiences with consent or you can use it in a mindful way with a friend or partner to explore consent through touch. You can check out BettyMartin.org for her three minute game exercise plus tons of other great videos on the wheel of consent. Another great exercise to use is the Sensate Touch hands exercise in my book *Unfuck Your Intimacy*.

The idea behind this exercise is that in any interaction, sexual or otherwise, there is a "doing to" person and a "doing for" person, and there are four quadrants of invvteraction within these two roles. It's

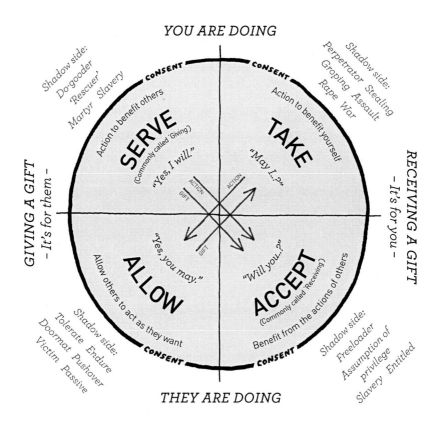

In any instance of touch, there are two factors: who is doing and who it's for. Those two factors combine in four ways (quadrants). Each quadrant presents its own challenges, lessons and joys.

The circle represents consent (your agreement). Inside the circle there is a gift given and a gift received. Outside the circle (without consent) the same action becomes stealing, abusing, etc.

© Dr. Betty Martin / www.bettymartin.org
You are welcome to share, including this diagram, with attribution (leave this paragraph in).

called the Wheel of Consent because we usually don't just play one of these roles but are constantly engaged in the give-and-take of everyday interactions.

The Doing-To Person Can Be Acting in One of Two Roles:

1) *The Serve* Role: An action to the benefit of others. The Serve role states "Yes, I will."*

In this role you are doing something for someone. The Serve role is not about your expectations (even the response you are expecting from the person you are serving). This is a true gift of action on your part, you are creating the space for another's choice and desire and fulfilling that desire when you are able to do so with an open mind and heart. Any action done for others with coercion or resentment is not a true serve role within the wheel of consent.

*The Serve role is often referred to as the "give" role, but the Allow role is also a form of giving, so serve is used here to delineate the difference

2) *The Take Role: An action to the benefit of yourself. The Take role asks "May I have?"*

In this role, you are doing something for you. The Take role is about asking someone else access to them after asking them their permission and limits around doing so. It is simply about your desires, not what they desire in return. This is a very difficult role for most of us, because it feels selfish. But within the wheel of consent, the take role allows others to open themselves to you while recognizing and crystalizing their own boundaries in the process.

The Doing-For Person Can Be Acting in One of Two Roles:

1) *The Allow Role: Letting others do what they want. The Allow role states "Yes you may."*

In this role, someone is doing something to you for their benefit. The Allow role is the other side of the Take role. In this role you are giving the gift of access to you. This is where you listen for an unhesitating "yes" from inside you. If you don't hear that voice, consider what you can wholeheartedly allow if other limits were involved and communicate those limits. The Allow role is not just about being open to others but discovering your own limits.

2) *The Accept* Role: Benefits from the actions of others. The Accept role asks "Will you?"*

YOUR SERVE ROLE EXPERIENCES:

YOUR TAKE ROLE EXPERIENCES:

In this role, someone is doing something, but the action is for you and not for them. The Accept role is the other side of the Serve role. This is a chance to really experience someone doing something that is truly for you. Think about what you really want them to do, and communicate that. If it changes, communicate the changes you would like. Ask clearly and directly (concrete as pavement) and focus on your experience of accepting rather than their experience of serving.

*The Accept role is commonly referred to as the receive role, but taking is also a form of receiving too, right?

The Shadow Side of the Consent Quadrants

T he term "shadow side" comes from Jungian psychology. The shadow side is more than just badness or evilness, though it can certainly be those things. Jung originally explained the shadow side as the aspects of our subconscious that we have not yet brought to light. In his book *Psychology and Religion*, he wrote:

"Everyone carries a shadow, and the less it is embodied in the individual's conscious life, the blacker and denser it is."

Jung understood our shadows as vestiges of our evolutionarily driven survival instincts. The shadow self isn't a bad thing in the least. Besides being the seat of our survival instincts, it is a font of creativity and greater understanding. But shadow integration (when we are aware of and accept our drives, without letting them rule us) is a continuous, lifelong process.

The blurring of consent is exactly where we can see the darker aspects of our shadow selves. So active, continuous consent isn't just a

**YOUR ALLOW ROLE
EXPERIENCES:**

**YOUR ACCEPT ROLE
EXPERIENCES:**

new-tangled buzzword, it's a conscious form of understanding and integrating our shadows so we can maintain healthy relationships and self-respect.

In an ideal situation, in the Serve role, you are the one *engaging in action* and giving a gift to the Accept role, who is actively accepting your action. In the Take role you are the one engaging in action while the person in the allow role is giving the gift of *allowing that action*. This isn't to say that some exchanges are better than others, anything happening within the circle happens with consent and like everything else in life, there are both positive and negative aspects to our interactions.

It is when we move out of the circle and into the shadow side of any of these roles that we move out of authentic consent.

- **The Serve Role Shadow Side:** Martyr, do-gooder, pushover, self-assigned slave, rescuer, codependent

- **The Take Role Shadow Side:** Assaulter, perpetrator, warmonger, rapist, thief

- **The Allow Role Shadow Side:** Victim, doormat, tolerator, passive

- **The Accept Role Shadow Side:** Freeloader, assumer, entitled

When we talk about violations of consent, we often discuss the shadow side of the Take role, but when we use the lens of Betty Martin's wheel of consent, we see that the dynamic of consent violations is far more complex than we commonly discuss.

And we likely have all fallen into shadow behaviors in at least one of the consent quadrants. My personal failing has been in the shadow side of the Serve role. The personality traits that led me to be a mental health professional also make it easy for me to fall into

SERVE SHADOW SIDE BEHAVIORS:

TAKE SHADOW SIDE BEHAVIORS:

ALLOW SHADOW SIDE BEHAVIORS:

ACCEPT SHADOW SIDE BEHAVIORS:

being a rescuer and a push-over. It's something that I struggled with throughout my 20s and early 30s, finally doing some active work around it in my own therapy.

What shadow sides have you noticed enacting in your own life? Make notes below.

Questions for Reflection

1) Are there any quadrant areas that you struggle to operate within comfortably?

2) Do you have any history with others violating your consent in overt or covert ways?

3) Did you realize that any of your experiences that you previously considered normal may have, in fact, been someone's problematic/shadow side behaviors?

4) Which shadow side behaviors do you need to do your own work around?

5) What behaviors would be more authentic to true consent?

6) Using an "If...Then..." create a plan around engaging in proactive behaviors if you find yourself slipping into old patterns?

7) Which shadow side behaviors are the responsibility of others in your life?

8) Using an "If...Then..." create a plan around establishing boundaries with others' behaviors when they interact with you based on old patterns?

CONCLUSION

I know. That was a lot. Like a ridiculous amount of a lot. It wasn't bad enough that we had to go into all the rape culture, we then had to talk about coercive control, manipulative people, and all kinds of other shitty and difficult topics.

Writing a lot of this zine made me feel like the entirety of the world is a dumpster fire. You may be feeling the same way after reading it.

The good news is, that I know better can happen and is happening. Having these conversations is public spaces is a sign of that. The fact that we even have the data that we have, means the monsters are no longer shadowy figures that we don't even know how to fight. Culture is changing and here is our opportunity to really do it right. It's not futile and I have some ideas of where we can begin.

Hopefully the wheel of consent exercise—and everything in this zine—helps you be more mindful and purposeful in your interactions with others. Most of us aren't used to having and expressing agency in our lives, so practicing autonomy and choice in an intentional ways can help us create huge shifts in how we interact with others while respecting them and ourselves.

APPENDIX
Sample Consent Contract

Since our contemporary conversation around consent started within the kink community, let's look at one of the more formal consent tools that has come from the aforementioned community. Some people may snicker at the idea, but a written consent contract doesn't exist for the purpose of earning extra-woke brownie points. They made legal sense for BDSM play, but even more so...they create a foundation and structure for a conversation about active, continuous consent. And that's not woke-ness...that's badass, thoughtful adulting.

I, , hereby declare under penalty of perjury that I am over 18 years old and am not under the influence of intoxicants or medications that inhibit my ability to affirm consent.

I further declare that this agreement is of my own free will and that neither I nor anyone near or dear to me has been threatened with negative consequences if I chose not to enter into this contract. _____

Both parties agree that this is a private agreement not to be disclosed to third parties except in case of accusation of sexual misconduct by an agreeing party.

If an agreeing party shows or makes public this agreement without accusation of sexual misconduct, it is agreed that they will be liable for damages for invasion of privacy.

By initialing, I agree to engage in all or some of the following consensual acts. _____

With the following individual(s)

_____

_____

_____

_____

Safer sex methods that I want utilized during these acts include:

_____

_____

_____

_____

At this time I do not intend to change my mind before the sex act or acts are over. However, if I do, it is further understood that when I say the words or make the signal (hand gesture, etc. all involved parties/partners agree to STOP INSTANTLY!

_____

_____

_____

Signed: _____

Date: _____

Signed:_____

Date: _____

Disclaimer: This sample contract does not constitute legal advice and is provided for educational purposes only. Check with legal counsel before entering into any agreement.

SUBSCRIBE!

For as little as $15 / month, you can
support a small, independent publisher
and get every book that we publish—
delivered to your doorstep!

www.Microcosm.Pub/BFF